Cognitive Behavioral Therapy for Depression

Discover How to Regain Energy and Motivation through Clear and Immediate Exercises to Overcome Depression and Finally Live a Happy Life

Lindsay Randell

Disclaimer

This book is designed to provide accurate and authoritative information in regard to the subject matter covered. By its sale, neither the publisher nor the author is engaged in rendering psychological or other professional services. If expert assistance or counseling is needed, the services of a competent professional should be sought.

Table of Contents

Introduction

Congratulations on purchasing *Cognitive Behavioral Therapy for Depression,* and thank you for doing so.

Depression is a common disorder in today's world. However, there is nothing to worry about as you will come across various ways in this book to deal with depression, overcome your negative thoughts, and also lead a better life. CBT, also known as cognitive behavioral therapy, is often considered the best treatment for depression. Generally, it is performed by therapists or mental health experts. But it can be done on your own as well. You will gain knowledge about how your feelings, thoughts, and actions are linked and also what can be done on your part to keep this positive and healthy cycle going. Negative thoughts are never a good thing for your life, and you will need to challenge them in every possible way to lead a better life.

Depression might turn out to be a tough thing to deal with, and so you will have to get hold of the tools, along with the skills, to master the art of dealing with the same. The main concept of CBT is that although some of our actions can be kept under control using conscious thoughts, others are the result of our unconscious thoughts. Thoughts and experiences of this nature stem from the environment where you spend the majority of your life. You will come to know about every important aspect of CBT in this guidebook and the ways you can benefit from it.

There are plenty of books on this subject on the market, thanks again for choosing this one! Every effort was made to ensure it is full of as much useful information as possible.Make sure lo leave a short review on Amazon if you enjoy it, i would really like to know your opinion!

Chapter 1:

What is CBT?

CBT or cognitive behavioral therapy is a form of treatment that is used for treating mental health issues. It can provide necessary help to people so that they can properly identify and change all forms of destructive or uneasy patterns of thinking. CBT can help in ending all such thoughts that might impart some sort of negative impact on your behaviors and emotions. The entire procedure of the therapy focuses on changing negative thought patterns that come with the power of worsening anxiety, depression, and various emotional difficulties. Spontaneous negative thoughts of this nature can easily have some form of detrimental influence on your overall mood. CBT helps in diagnosing all these thoughts, challenge them, and then replace the same with objective and positive thoughts.

There are various other therapy and treatment options available for the treatment of depression and some other serious mental health issues. However, the effectiveness showcased by CBT makes it the best possible option that is available today for the treatment of mental health issues. It is used for treating other problems as well, such as panic disorder, anxiety, sleep disorder, and many others. Let us start with the history of CBT.

CBT And Its History

It was during the 1960s when CBT was introduced for the first time. Aaron Beck, a psychiatrist, first noticed that certain types of thinking could easily result in emotional problems. He identified all those thoughts as automatic negative thoughts and started developing the entire process of CBT. All other types of behavioral therapies concentrated only on punishments, reinforcements, and associations for modifying behaviors. However, CBT provided the required help to properly address the way in which thoughts and feelings actually affect all our behaviors. From that time, this form of therapy is regarded as one of the most effective forms of treatment for various types of mental health conditions.

Types Of CBT

There are various types of CBT, along with several behavioral therapies, which might also be included under the umbrella of CBT. Some of the most common types of CBT include:

- CPT or Cognitive Processing Therapy
- DBT or Dialectical Behavior Therapy
- CT or Cognitive Therapy
- REBT or Rational Emotive Behavior Therapy
- Stress Inoculation Training
- Self-Instructional Training

CBT is often short-term. It is probably in reference to the traditional modes of psychotherapy which involves several sessions of therapy per week for several years. It has been found that psychological problems, like OCD or obsessive-compulsive disorder, panic attacks, depression, PTSD or post-traumatic stress disorder, and various others can be treated with the help of CBT within eight to twenty weeks. BPD or borderline personality disorder can be treated within fifty-two weeks. While the related protocols of treatment in all such studies come with a certain number of sessions along with a defined clinical population, there is a great amount of flexibility in practice. It indicates that with the proper assessment, a therapist can easily tailor the therapy in accordance with the needs of the patient.

Also, several people opting for this therapy might have more than one single issue that needs to be addressed, such as OCD and depression. In such a case, the total number of sessions might take some more than what a specific protocol stipulates. While each of the types of CBT comes with some sort of different approach, they all work for addressing the underlying patterns of thoughts that lead to psychological distress.

CBT And Its Uses

CBT or cognitive behavior therapy is widely used for helping people with some specific problems as a short-term treatment. It also teaches patients to focus on their current thoughts and beliefs. It is used extensively for treating various mental health issues.

Depression

Whenever it comes to the aspect of depression, CBT is often considered the most effective option of treatment. All of us suffer from depression. However, if you feel sad or low, that cannot be considered as being depressed. In general, depression gets triggered by a series of events of stressful nature. Events of this type will generally leave you back with a feeling as if no other option is left and the entire world is against you. When all of this turns out to be chronic, it might also push a person to the cliff of suicide as the only solution. In case you go for therapy and your mental health expert figures out that you are having suicidal thoughts, he/she will take some necessary measures to ensure that you are safe. It is important to keep in mind that the majority of people live under the pressure of stress at several points in their daily lives. Well, you can consider this as the result of the current advancements of the technological world. It prevents people from breaking free from their day-to-day routines, and the only thing known to them is work.

Stress of this nature can easily lead to negative thoughts. In fact, it can make you feel low. But keep in mind that all such things cannot be collectively termed as depression. Before you point out yourself as being depressed, you will need to be checked by a mental health expert or a therapist. CBT is generally used for treating depression cases as it can very easily find out the reasons why it is taking the shape of some serious issues. General treatments will involve several consultation periods that will allow the therapist and you to properly talk about the reasons behind your behaviors of depression. All forms of influences and issues that you have come through in your entire life till the present moment will be properly studied to bring the primary issue to the surface. CBT helps in dealing with the problems of depression simply by isolating all forms of pre-disposed patterns of thoughts and behaviors, which ultimately leads to a cycle of depression.

By proper isolation of your thoughts and reactions and then changing all of them, all your negative thoughts can be avoided quite easily, which generally drives you crazy during periods of depression. The procedure of treatment is natural, and it generally lasts for a lifetime after successful completion.

Sleeping problems

In a recent study, it has been stated that there might be a direct connection between some mental health issues and sleeping problems. CBT has showcased various positive effects on all those individuals who tend to suffer from irregular and poor sleeping patterns. In fact, lack of sleep can also result in several serious alterations in your regular life that also includes tiredness during the course of the day. Lack of sleep will also prevent you from completing all your work on time. There are various reasons behind irregular patterns of sleeping or insomnia.

- One of the primary reasons behind insomnia is stress. It will never allow your mind to rest and relax. Constantly being wired can make the task of sleeping quite hard for you.

- Some types of physical illness and medication might affect your ability to get proper sleep.

- Another factor that might affect your sleeping pattern is your sleeping area. It might be the case that your sleeping area has too much or too little light, constant surrounding noise, or an uncomfortable bed.

- Issues that are related to mental health can make you feel scared to fall asleep.

CBT has shown some great results in dealing with all such issues and also brings back a good night's sleep.

Panic disorder

There are certain individuals who might be preoccupied with panic, even with the simplest events or situations. Well, there might be no real reason behind the panic, or it might also be linked to some stimulus. While panic is a form of natural response that is related to extreme incidents, panic disorder is all about repeated and regular incidents of panic. In fact, it might take the shape of something serious, like scared of stepping out of the house. Panic is all about a sudden surge of emotions that can be linked to chemical responses in the presence of excessive danger. It involves the stimulus of fight or flee. You can regard this as a survival instinct that has been a part of human nature for as long as our evolution.

People who suffer from panic disorders will experience the same nature of stimulus as others. However, when they need to make a decision whether to fight or flee and experience an adrenaline rush, they will get overwhelmed due to all their emotions. Some of the most common signs that are related to panic disorder are sweating, nausea, heart palpitations, and trembling. Well, there is no need to get admitted to a hospital when you have an attack most of the time. Panic attacks won't be harming you physically. However, the panic attacks might take some frightening structure at times. In the majority of cases, the related panic tends to stem from certain events and behaviors from earlier days or childhood where the mind gets programmed to react in some definite ways. It might also develop from behavioral patterns of parents where they try to stop their children from doing certain actions without feeling the need to explain why it is not acceptable.

The mind will automatically link itself with some scenarios and actions with negative responses of this nature. The ultimate result will be panic attacks whenever you face similar situations. You might come preoccupied with panic in case you possess some types of genes. In a recent study, it has been found that upbringing can also affect panic attacks. CBT is used for reducing your fear of some stimulus gradually. It also involves retracing of all forms of influences, which resulted in responses of extreme nature. It will provide you with the needed help to change the way in which you actually think of them. It will ultimately affect the response coming from your side that you tend to have in the same nature of situations. Well, it is important to seek help to treat this disorder as it comes with the power of affecting your abilities in extreme ways.

CBT is also put into use for the treatment of various other issues.

- Addictions

- Anger issues

- Phobias

- Anxiety

- Personality disorder

- Eating disorder

- Bipolar disorder

CBT And Its Impact

The primary concept behind CBT is that our thoughts and feelings tend to play some essential role in determining our behavior. For example, an individual who just keeps thinking of plane accidents, crash on the runway, or some other air disaster might give his best to maintain distance from air travel. The aim of CBT is to teach people that although it is not possible to control everything in life, they can still take control of how they deal with and interpret several aspects around them. In the last few years, CBT has turned out to be a popular topic among consumers of mental health and also treatment professionals. There are certain reasons behind all of this.

- As we try to be aware of the negative and unrealistic thoughts that tend to dampen our overall feelings and mood, we can start to concentrate on healthier thought patterns.

- It acts as an effective and superb short-term treatment option.

- It helps in dealing with a wide range of emotional distress where there is no need for psychotropic medication.

- It is affordable in comparison to other options of therapy.

CBT And Its Strategies

We all often experience certain thoughts or feelings that tend to reinforce faulty beliefs. Such beliefs might gradually result in problematic behaviors that can easily affect our life, including family, work, relationships, and academics.

Identification of negative thoughts

It is an important thing to learn how thoughts, feelings, and situations result in maladaptive behaviors. The process might turn out to be tough, especially for those who fight with introspection. But as the ultimate result, it can lead to self-discovery as well as insights that are essential parts of the entire process of treatment.

Setting up goals

Setting up goals is a very important step in the overall process of recovery from any kind of mental illness. It can deliver you with the needed help to bring in certain changes for improving the condition of your health and life. During the sessions of CBT, a mental health expert or therapist can provide you with the necessary help with the various goal-setting skills. You will come to learn how you can identify all your goals, differentiate between short-term goals and long-term goals, develop measurable, attainable, relevant, and time-based goals, and focus on the overall process, along with the ultimate outcome.

Practicing brand new skills

It is necessary to start practicing new skills that you can use for various real-world situations. For example, a person suffering from substance abuse disorder can start with new skills of coping and practicing new ways to stay away from or to deal with social situations that might result in some kind of serious relapse.

Self-monitoring

Often referred to as diary work, self-monitoring is an essential aspect of CBT that involves symptom tracking, behavior tracking, along with tracking of experiences at times. As you opt for the therapy, you will need to share all of these with the mental health expert or therapist. Providing all this information to the therapist will help him/her to deliver you with the best form of treatment. For example, in the case of eating disorders, it might include keeping track of eating habits along with the thoughts or feelings that were present at the time of consumption of the food.

CBT And Its Benefits

CBT comes with various types of benefits that can be gradually identified.

- It is as effective as any form of medication that is put into use for treating certain chronic mental health issues. In a recent study, it has been found that about 8% of the people in the US tend to suffer from chronic depression each year. Some of the most common symptoms that can be widely found are loss of interest in all those things that were enjoyed previously, isolation, low energy, and development of various physical diseases. When CBT is properly followed, the negative thinking patterns can be easily reconstructed.

- The therapy takes lesser time to be completed in comparison to other types of therapy. Patients undergoing CBT will need to go for individual sessions that last for thirty minutes to one hour. The overall timeframe of each session will depend on the related problems. If you opt for CBT, you will need to meet your mental health expert once every week or once every alternate week. In the majority of CBT cases, they last for approximately twenty weeks or sometimes less than that. The best thing about CBT is that it will let you experience the overall result within a short period of time.

- You will come across several sessions and tools in CBT that get used relying on the issues. Various tools are put into use for each patient as they work in the direction of restructuring their thought patterns. In fact, you can opt for group sessions that will show you that you are not the only one suffering from depression or other mental health issues.

- In CBT, your therapist will not tell you what needs to be done. He/she will work in collaboration with you to find out the most suitable solution for all your issues. It indicates that you will need to determine the issues on a personal level and invest everything that you have for making the needed changes in your life. It will allow you to find out various solutions for different problems. You can think of CBT as a collaborative effort. You will come to find more accountability in the entire process. As you jump into something with a supportive partner by your side, your overall chances of achieving the same will automatically get doubled.

- CBT can be used for any age group. Both adults and children can opt for CBT and also benefit from the same when used properly. The expectations for any age group will also be the same. As long as you have the capacity and willingness to bring about certain changes in your life, CBT will help you with several solutions that you can put into use for the treatment of all your pre-existing problems. Also, taking some time to discuss any situation or issue will show effective results. It is primarily because most of us tend to internalize all our tough situations. It only results in lots of suffering. CBT will help you to trust yourself and break through the continuous cycle of negative thoughts.

Chapter 2:

Things To Keep In Mind Before You Start

CBT or cognitive behavioral therapy is a kind of talking therapy that helps in combating various types of mental health issues, like depression, anxiety, phobias, and OCD. It works by altering the way you behave and think. Well, it is also carried out in group sessions, as we have already discussed earlier. It is recommended by general physicians as the best non-medical solution in order to treat mental health conditions. It works on the theory that our beliefs, thoughts, and behaviors are connected to each other, and in case they are negative in nature or gets fueled by depression or anxiety; they can push us in the direction of a downward spiral. Everything that you will learn in CBT is about breaking through this dreading cycle also training your mind to think in a different way. Well, it will not readily help you in getting rid of your mental health issues; however, it will provide you with practical ways in which you can manage and cope with the same.

For some individuals, the concept of group sessions might seem very daunting, and the 'therapy' term is enough for putting others off altogether. It is nothing like that in actuality, and you will have to keep certain things in mind right before you start with the same. Let's have a look at them.

Is It The Right Choice For You?

CBT can be used for anything starting from depression, anxiety, phobias, self-esteem issues, trauma, and ADHD, to problems in relationships like unrealistic expectations from partners or poor communication. In simple terms, it is an issue that includes behaviors and thoughts; CBT has a definite treatment approach for the same. Well, is it the right choice for you? That is surely a tough question. Do all your problems concern how you behave and think? For instance, are you finding yourself shopping online mindlessly, or are you ruminating about a breakup from the past? If so, then you could surely benefit from the approach of CBT. In case you are more concerned about your life's meaning or purpose, there might be other options that will fit better in your case.

Is There Any Need To Open Up

During your group sessions of CBT, you are not needed to open up regarding your personal anxieties unless and until you want to. In fact, your therapist might ask you not to go into details regarding your personal experiences so that he/she can get through all forms of content that can be useful for everyone at the time of the session. However, if you are willing to provide personal anecdotes while talking about something specific or while asking a question, that is absolutely fine.

Why Is CBT So Popular?

One of the main reasons why CBT is so widely used and popular is because it has been extensively studied. It can be regarded as a good modality to study as it emphasizes direct, brief, and solution-oriented interventions. In simple terms, the goal is to make measurable and clear changes in behaviors and thoughts, which acts like a goldmine for all the researchers. It also indicates that you can see quick results. As a great percentage of people are suffering from some sort of depression and anxiety, being capable of gently challenging people to directly face all their fears and establish new ways to relate to their thoughts is a main area of the work. CBT helps by providing tools that encourage people to opt for something very unpleasant – confront all those things that are avoided.

What Really Happens in CBT Sessions?

CBT is a common form of psychotherapy. So, you can expect the initial sessions to be like any other form of therapy – discussing your therapy goals, a review of all your problems, and your past. Right after that, you will need to talk about all those struggles that you encounter and formulate effective responses altogether. The patients bring in all those problems that they want to overcome or all those situations that they find stressful. The patient and therapist will work closely to create a plan of action. A plan of action means they determine the problematic behaviors or thoughts, determine a definite way to alter them, and then develop certain strategies to implement all related changes in the next week. It is where 'homework' comes into the picture.

What Is Homework?

CBT is concentrated on providing an easy, quick, and effective symptom reduction, which can be done best by application of the techniques all throughout the week and not only at the time of the session. Generally, homework includes maintaining an emotion and thought journal during the course of the week, relaxation exercises, opting for worksheets that aim at certain growth areas, reading books that apply to the issues, or opting for situations in order to apply new approaches. For instance, you might want to keep track of all your meet-up events that tend to challenge you to deal with your fears while you apply your new techniques of relaxation. Or, say a major factor in your depression is your internal self-talk of negative nature. You keep beating and belittling yourself on a constant loop.

You and your therapist might discuss a CBT technique known as thought stopping. In this, you will need to disrupt the flow of your negative thoughts by saying "Stop" in your mind as you redirect all your thoughts into something of a more positive nature, such as an affirmation. Your homework might include practicing this very technique once every day until you for the next session. In the next session, you and your therapist will opt for debriefing, evaluate those things that worked and that did not, and then tweak the entire process for the next session.

What Is The Duration Of The Treatment?

One of the primary highlights of CBT is that it is concentrated on discarding symptoms as soon as possible, typically within a time range of few weeks to some months. Indeed, patients rarely have only one issue to deal with this therapy, so the length will rely on the severity and number of the issues. However, brevity is the only key to this approach. It brings up one of the main differences between other therapy options and CBT. In most types of therapies, why, how, and what questions are generally asked. Why questions are not that productive. Other approaches of treatment tend to spend a lot of time digging deep and finding out why you feel anxious, depressed, or have a low level of self-esteem. But in the case of CBT, it tries to stick to the current behaviors and thoughts.

Instead of examining 'why' you are scared of snakes, it focuses on reducing the fear. While some individuals are satisfied with the reduction of their symptoms, there are people who just want to know about why they exist. For all such people, deeper treatment approaches such as psychodynamic therapy will be more useful.

What Is The Cost Of CBT, And Is It Covered By Insurance?

CBT is a leg of psychotherapy. So, in case your insurance company covers behavioral medicine or psychotherapy, it would cover the majority, if not all, of the treatment. Generally, CBT sessions cost approximately $150 or more than that in private practice. The time length that is needed for someone will depend on the severity of the issues, and that might also affect the overall costing. However, it provides quicker solutions and so it will be cheaper in comparison to other treatment options in the long run.

Are There Are Any Possible Down Sides?

There are patients who have the feeling that they want their therapy to be a place where they can come and process all their experiences along with some facilitation by the concerned therapist. Their primary goal might not be to deal with any particular problematic habit or symptom; however, more about a long-term relationship and general growth with their therapist. It might be the case that they want to explore their dreams and memories with the proper guidance of the therapist. Provided that CBT is a practical and direct kind of therapy, it might not be helpful for a person who is seeking this nature of relational and deep work. With that said, there are several skilled therapists who are quite flexible with the overall approach and can also easily adjust in order to meet the requirements of various types of clients.

There are certain downsides that you will need to keep in mind before you opt for CBT.

- The entire change might turn out to be tough. In the starting, there are patients who might suggest that as they determine some of their thoughts and behaviors as irrational or unhealthy, only being aware of such thoughts isn't going to make it easy for them to change.

- The entire setup of CBT is quite structured. It does not focus on any kind of underlying unconscious resistance to change like other types of approaches, for example, psychoanalytic psychotherapy. It is suited for all those people who are comfortable with a structured and focused type of approach. The concerned mental health expert or therapist will also take up some beneficial instructional role.

- People who are dealing with unhealthy and irrational patterns of thinking need to be willing to alter. For the success of the therapy and for the best effects of the same, the concerned patient will need to spend some time analyzing their thoughts and feelings. Such types of self-analysis and homework might be quite tough. But it is a great way to learn how your internal states can have some sort of impact on your outward behavior.

The first step that you will need to take in getting better is properly recognizing that you are having certain issues or problems. As you have opted for this book, you are surely facing something. Most of us try to downplay all our problems and face difficulties in reaching out for help. One of the main advantages of opting for CBT on your own is that you will not require to get over that very hurdle. It is also essential to keep in mind that depression and other mental health conditions are serious illnesses that are possible to be treated. Depression is nothing but a chemical imbalance in the brain. CBT helps in the reduction of negative thoughts, live healthier, and develop better habits; thus, providing the brain with the resources to heal on its own. You have nothing to do with your depression as it might be the result of various factors.

For getting the most out of CBT, start with a journal. Even in case you do not have the habit of writing or you are not much familiar with a journal, it will act as an essential tool in the path of your recovery. You might take some time to get habituated to the same, and you might even get some odd feelings while writing down so many things. But it is for your own good. As you start doing it, you can notice immediate improvements in your overall mental health. It will turn out to be a part of your routine eventually, and you cannot skip the same for a day. You can opt for any kind of journal that you want. The aim is to write down all those things that you feel and think.

Chapter 3:
Identifying The Problems

Identification of problems is an important step in the entire process of CBT. The perfect way of describing the working of CBT is to get knowledge about how a mental health expert or therapist might go through with any patient. The overall process of identification of the problems as well as solving the same is carried out in several stages. We will discuss the various stages in which the problems are identified in this chapter.

1st Stage: Assessment

During the initial stages of CBT, your therapist will give their all to find out the type of problems that are trying to make your life troublesome. In fact, he/she will also try to explore all your set goals – what do you want to receive after the therapy ends? Your CBT therapist will carry out an assessment to gather knowledge about all or some of these:

- Opting for open and direct questions to help the concerned patient open about his/her problems. For instance, "You can frankly tell why you are sitting here," "What are the things that have taken up the shape of problems recently?"

- The therapist would develop a list of problems in collaboration with the patient. It would also include thinking properly regarding the essentiality of the problems. For instance, "Now that we have a proper list of all the problems, can we arrange them from the most problematic ones to the least problematic ones so that we can ensure how much they interfere with your daily life?"

- The mental health expert or therapist would want to develop specific and measurable goals in cooperation with the patient. It is done by focusing on those behaviors that the concerned patient wants to alter. For instance, "What would you have been doing in a different way in case all your problems did not have the tags of problems anymore?"

- Another way in which a therapist might try to determine the problems is by opting for structured interviews or questionnaires. It will help in assessing the presence or absence of symptoms or difficulties.

- Your therapist might ask you several questions regarding your current and earlier suicidal thoughts and actions. For instance, "Have you ever had the thought of putting your life to an end or even hurting your own self?"

Focusing on specific events: 1st assessment technique

The best way of learning about the problems of the patients is by paying proper attention to some events that happened recently. In simple terms, the mental health expert would try to determine absolute details such as, "Yesterday whenever I came across someone in the street who seemed like an attacker; I was filled with fear at the spot" instead of, "I feel low all the time that I am not sure whether this life is of any possible worth." It will need a great amount of work to extract proper details from the latter example. The main reason why CBT focuses on specific life events is that all our lives are developed for some moments that are chained together in one place. All of us live our lives by one moment after the other. The same goes for all our feelings. In fact, all of us have the habit of telling certain stories to ourselves, such as, "I had the most boring and the worst day of life today."

But the chances are high that the entire day had only certain boring moments and was mostly filled with excitement. In case we shift all our attention to our thoughts and behaviors, all of these will keep going moment by moment. All that we will do is end up not paying attention to the essential parts of we just keep glossing over all the details. Your past problems might not be an issue anymore is the primary cause why the procedure of the therapy focuses on those aspects that are being seen as mere problems now. When bad or devastating things happened in the past, the suffering or difficulty which we try to relieve from takes place in the present moment. One of the major assumptions made by the process of CBT is that all those things that happen in the current moment dedicate to the sufferings.

Breaking down each moment into essential components: 2nd assessment technique

Right after you are done with the task of discovering the latest and specific event, it is now time to separate the same into various small and manageable components. It will include:

- **Cognitions:** What went through your mind at the moment?

- **Situation:** Who was there? What happened exactly? What was the exact location? What did it happen?

- **Trigger:** What was going on right before the issue?

- **Body sensations:** What feelings or sensations you determined in your body?

- **Emotions:** What were the feelings?

- **Actions or responses:** How did you respond? What did you do to cope with the problem?

The main reason why CBT therapists focus on assessments by dividing the events into several components is that the main approach of CBT believes all such components are interlinked to each other. One component will surely affect the other in plenty of ways. Trying to develop a proper sense of all available connections is known as case conceptualization.

2nd Stage: Formulation Of The Case

It is completely a different approach to address persisting problems. But in order to determine the proper solution, we will need to:

- Properly understand what is contributing to the problem to stay for such a long time

- Finding plenty of ways to end the same

CBT therapists tend to use a technique termed case conceptualization or case formulation. It is all about understanding the ways in which a problem operates. The formulation is as simple as a bunch of hypotheses or a simple model. A CBT therapist will establish their own hypotheses and will also explore if the patient has any available set of hypotheses. After this, he/she will figure out definite paths in collaboration with the patient to determine the correctness of the available hypotheses.

CBT concentrates on relationships and consequences

While discussing problems of any kind, your therapist will concentrate on collecting information regarding – where and when the problem initiates, the related triggers, body sensations, behaviors, and emotions that lead to the problem. The next step is to determine the existing relationships between the available components. Generally:

- Everything that you see can act as a trigger for all your mind thoughts. Some of the common triggers for resulting in thoughts include body sensations, incidents, every possible thing present around you, other types of thoughts, and memories. In fact, you can think about any small possible thing. So, it can be stated that anything can take the shape of a possible trigger for all your thoughts.

- All the actions showcased by you come with some consequences. You can link this to Newton's third law – "Every possible action has an equal and opposite reaction." All actions are the same; everything that you do in life also comes along with various consequences. Some of the portions of the consequences might be intentional in nature, while some might be not. A question like, "What were the consequences of that action?" is a common step in CBT. Proper analysis of the consequences provides the therapists of CBT with the required help to find out why the problem patterns just persist longer than otherwise expected.

- All your thoughts result in feelings slowly. An essential insight of CBT is that the way we opt for interpretation of certain situations might affect how we actually feel for them. Such interpretations can take place quickly and automatically. In fact, they might get affected by various other things or events that happened in the past.

CBT concentrates on all those things that make problems persist

A fire needs three primary components to keep burning: oxygen, heat, and fuel. The longer these components are available, the fire will keep burning. With this very idea, firefighters can determine which of the components to target. Depending on the overall nature of the fire, firefighters will make up their mind to:

- Cut off the supply of oxygen by the use of CO_2

- Spray water for cutting off the available heat

- Discard the available fuel

The treatment of CBT also examines problems in more or less the same way: the primary focus is on the components that tend to maintain the problem in its place. Just like fire, it is not important to determine the factors that ignited it. But you will need to make sure of all those things that allow it to keep burning. CBT therapists come with proper training to aim all their attention on any form of sequence that seems like being in a constant loop. Well, there are various ways in which human problems can be taken proper care of. Some common factors that might permit the problems to be in their place are:

- **Biased memory:** It is all about recalling only a part or portion of the entire story. People who suffer from depression, anxiety, or other mental health conditions can easily remember all sorts of threatening details

32

automatically. Also, people who suffer from depressive disorder might have 'over general' memory. They might also find it tough to recall some events.

- **Avoidance:** It can be both external and internal. One of the problems that result from avoidance is that it will give us any chance of figuring out how we could have dealt with the overall problem in case we did not avoid the same. For instance, "Harry was always so anxious regarding something catastrophic taking place that he decided not to even leave the house. In fact, he tried to stay away from the door."

- **Safety behaviors:** It involves all those things that we try to maintain a safe distance from that we think might turn out to be a catastrophe. Just like avoidance, the primary problem that comes along with safety behaviors is that they might prevent us from determining that the negative outcomes might not have taken place ever.

- **Reinforcement:** All of us have the habit of repeating all those things that leave us back with some sort of good feeling. In fact, it might be the case that the overall behavior is not good for us for the long term.

- **Biased attention:** Your attention will seem like being biased when you see only one portion of the event or incident. Well, the basic problem is that we all try to pay attention only to failures. We just do not pay enough attention to the successes. Every one of us tends to be biased with an image of our own selves.

- **Self-criticism:** It is about telling yourself all you have done, or you are. In certain cases, a small area of self-criticism might seem motivating. But in most cases, it is carried out in the setting of punishment in place of being encouraging.

- **Repetitive thinking:** It is about sticking by the existing and persisting problems, in addition to asking questions like, "Why is my entire life like this?" It has been found that 'why' questions are not that helpful like 'how' questions.

How all the pieces fit together?

It has been discovered that the maintaining factors might just come together in certain ways for developing problems or issues. Let's have a detailed look at several common problems, along with the factors that allow them to persist.

Anxiety

People who suffer from panic attacks experience body sensations of ambiguous nature at times. They get the feeling that the presence of all such sensations is the indicator of something terrific. Such type of thinking results in strong reactions of emotions in addition to some attempts to cope, which are of understandable nature. The avoidance, selective attention, and avoidance tend to act as important maintaining factors for panic.

Mixed Problems

There are certain individuals who struggle with more than one type of problem at once. Well, the concept of CBT is flexible in nature. Using the same nature of building blocks can provide us with a framework in order to understand the persisting problems so that our framework can be developed.

Depression

People who experience low moods all the time showcase alterations in their behaviors in addition to their patterns of thinking. Changes of this nature allow depression to stick to its place.

3rd Stage: Monitoring Of Symptoms

After the patient and therapist have determined the problem or problems to concentrate on, along with a proper idea of the components that are helping the problem to be in its place, the CBT process concentrates on symptom monitoring, besides the actual problems. Just like our thoughts might result in being biased, the impressions about whether the process of CBT will be useful might also come under the effect of bias. CBT therapists make some assumptions about the functioning of the process. Also, it can be easily mistaken. The bias of this type can be easily dealt with by measuring all the problems, besides the symptoms, on a regular basis. It even includes checking with the concerned patient daily regarding what they think of the therapy's effectiveness. Monitoring of the symptoms is not at all a tough thing to do as it involves keeping count of how often something or problems occur.

For instance, keeping a proper count of how many times or how often a person suffers from panic attacks.

4th Stage: Techniques For The Change

After a successful assessment of the problems, determination of the goals, and finding out why the problems exist, now it is time for some action. Sometimes, the case conceptualization stage alone can perform single-handedly to bring in the necessary motivation to change. People might feel relieved by discussing some of their problems or issues, might feel helpful by getting knowledge about the way it operates, and opt for certain important changes in their lives.

Techniques to alter how you feel by changing everything that you think

An important intervention in the process of CBT is to deliver the patients with support to understand and change the patterns that are not much useful in addition to the type of thinking. One of the basic ways in which CBT therapists help the suffering patients to change how they think is by providing them with CBT worksheets. It really helps in developing the base of their thought monitoring besides the practice of modification of thoughts. The very first step in changing what we think is to figure out what enters our minds. It is often referred to as thought monitoring. The next important step is to study the accuracy, along with the helpfulness of such thoughts, once the concerned patients can determine the negative thoughts. It is termed cognitive restructuring.

Identification Of Automatic Thoughts

Some of our feelings might feel predictable at certain times, whereas others might feel puzzling. Sometimes we feel certain emotions like out of the blue, too tough for the things that are currently going on. The key to properly understand all your feelings is to determine the thoughts that are linked to them. Thoughts come with the power of influencing all our experiences in addition to emotional experiences. Automatic thoughts are all those types of thoughts that crop up in our minds suddenly and automatically at any point of the day. The majority of times, we are not even aware of having such thoughts. But with the help of a little bit of instruction and practice, we can easily learn how to identify all such thoughts. As the ultimate result, we will get the chance to control our mood and behavior in a much better way.

Why pay attention to thoughts?

Human minds are like machines that just keep processing various types of thoughts. It also helps in the creation and sifting through a wide range of ideas every day. In case we try to attend all of them, we will just get flooded with a variety of information. The majority of thoughts enters the brain and leaves the same without us having any kind of idea regarding the same. Human minds are quite efficient in filtering out the thoughts that are not much useful and try to concentrate on those thoughts that are more salient. The entire process tends to function well the majority of the time. But sometimes, we just try to focus on the less essential information while kicking out the important ones—for instance, a review of job performance. We tend to filter out all forms of praise and focus on all those aspects where improvement is necessary. It is termed negative filtering. It is all about filtering out every possible thing except for the negative nature of the information.

The example here can highlight a powerful and very common dynamic: automatic thoughts come along with the potential of triggering various types of negative emotions. In general, we try to pay attention to all such emotions instead of the thoughts that actually act as the trigger. However, in the majority of cases, automatic thoughts tend to play some essential role in determining the way we actually feel and not the situation alone. As you start learning to examine all such thoughts, you will gain the power to better understand and deal with emotions. You will be able to modulate all of them right before they take the shape of something intense or overwhelming.

How can identification be made?

There are individuals who tend to find this skill a tough thing to master at first; however, they can get a catch of the same quite easily. The key to properly identify automatic thoughts is by determining all those things that come into your mind when any kind of emotion arises. For example, John found on social media that his friend Ron has arranged a small party with his friends where he is not invited. John will surely start feeling a pit in his stomach and properly identify his emotion as sadness. At that very moment, John asked himself, "What is going through all my mind?" He can easily identify the following thoughts:

- No one ever invites me anywhere.

- Ron no longer likes me as a friend.

- No one likes me as a friend.

Provided the extreme extent of all the thoughts, a proper feeling of sadness can be determined. By opting for writing down all the thoughts, John was capable of processing the thoughts differently and also determine the extent of all those thoughts. The overall exercise also allowed him to see that he was opting for some broad assumptions, which he did not try to believe. After some point of time, John started feeling better, and his sadness got lifted. The overall process of thought recognition is termed metacognition. It is a useful process that provides needed help in the development of awareness, besides an understanding of all the thoughts. As we just saw in the example, being aware of the thought processes can provide us with the needed help to develop a distance from all forms of cognitive responses and also reevaluate the same.

It is a tough thing to overstate how powerful this very tool can be for changing our feelings and behaviors. One more possible way of uncovering all your hidden thoughts is by asking, "What are the possible parts of all this, and why?" In such a case, the most probable answer is that John believes he never gets invited to anything, and it is quite hard to conclude that no one around him likes his presence. If all of the discussed methods fail to work for you, you can opt for identifying the emotions and then try to work in the backward direction.

Identification Of Intrusive Thoughts

Having obsessive as well as negative ideas in mind might result in being a great suffering source. It belongs to all those things that come with the power of easily intensifying the dangerous cycle of depression and anxiety. You might keep digging yourself in your own hole as you give your best to surround yourself with images and impulses, besides all forms of unhelpful reasoning that might easily cloud your overall sense of control. In such a case, listening to, "Calm down! You have nothing to worry about as all such things have not yet happened" will not help. No matter you like the actual fact or not, but our minds are more or less like a factory that keeps giving out new ideas. But everything that gets produced by the mind cannot help us attaining all our

39

goals or even make us feel a bit better. All of us come through such absurd and not so helpful ideas every possible day. However, under normal and cool conditions, we tend not to provide such reasoning with lots of power. Instead of that, we just give priority to encouraging and helpful thoughts.

How to deal with intrusive thoughts?

In order to deal with intrusive thoughts, you will need to master certain techniques.

Thought Records

It will allow you to apply some form of logic to all forms of mental processes. Suppose a friend of yours is always scared of losing his job. He will get obsessed with the thought that the management is not happy with his work. The cycle will result in some self-fulfilling prophecy. By trying to determine all those things that he might do wrong within a very short period of time, he will end up making that mistake. For getting a better sense of coherence, balance, and control, you can start creating records of your invasive thoughts. All that you will need to do is to write down all forms of negative ideas and thoughts that emerge in your mind. After that, you will only need to work on the actual truth.

Hierarchy of Concerns

Intrusive thoughts can be compared with smoke from a huge chimney. It is the heat of something that keeps burning inside us. The internal fire is the compilation of all sorts of unresolved problems that just keep worsening gradually with time. The initial step in controlling the overall concentration of your thoughts, anguish, and feelings is clarifying all of them. You will need to arrange your concerns on a scale that ranges from low to high. It can be done by first writing down all those issues that tend to concern you. It is more or less like brainstorming, where you will need to visualize the present chaos deep inside you. After this, give your all for establishing a hierarchy. Try to start with all those that you think of as mere problems. Conclude the hierarchy with those things that tend to leave you anxious and stressed. Once you have a visual order in front of yourself, now it is time to reflect on each point deeply. You will need to think of them rationally besides coming up with some sort of solution for each of them.

Preventing Intrusive Thoughts

No matter you want it or not, there will be some situations in life that will keep tempting you to jump into the trench of intrusive thoughts again. The best way to pay attention to all such situations is by maintaining a diary. Opting for something too easy and simple, like writing down your feelings and thoughts each day, will allow you to be more attentive and conscious of all those things that are present around you. All you need to do is to keep writing all those things that come to your mind. You will need to describe the situations when you experienced certain specific feelings. There will be people, events, or habits that will make you lose all your control. When you make it a habit to keep a record of your entire day, you will start seeing things in their actual form. You will gain the power to prevent yourself from developing some form of negative reaction to them.

Chapter 4:
Feelings, Actions, And Thoughts

The primary idea behind CBT is that the world around us cannot be controlled; however, we can control the way we react towards the same. For doing so, we will need to master the cycle that lies between our feelings, actions, and thoughts. Each one of these has some kind of effect on the other. If one or more than one of these tends to come from a negative place, the entire cycle will turn out to be negative. The aim of CBT is to alter at least any one of these to positive, and thus it will affect the other two as well.

The Brain Is A Complex Organ

When something takes place to you or around you, the brain tries to process the same almost immediately and then decides whether it is something that requires any kind of action or something that develops another thought within seconds. In case the brain decides that instant action is required, it will pass the information to the amygdala for activating the flight, fight, or freeze response. Although we do not have the same kind of frequent form of physical threats that earlier human beings used to, our brain treats stress and the modern-day ' dangers' in the exact same way as if a large beast is running behind us. Amygdala is the part of the brain that has been the longest around in respect to evolution. Right before any modern-day tools or technology came into being, human beings had to rely on the split-second response for survival.

In case a human being was in danger of being ripped off by a tiger, the amygdala would send signals for decreasing any form of cognitive activity, increase the rates of breathing and heart, make the muscles ready for movement, and just give the adrenaline level a shot. During the earlier days, all of this was essential to survive. In today's age, the flight, fight, or freeze response is no longer that useful. Human beings rarely fall for such situations, and the overall reaction does more amount of harm than good. People suffering from depression and anxiety tend to experience such reactions frequently and also to situations that cannot be considered to be normally threatening. It is where the automatic thoughts tend to come from. Although the human brain is complex in nature, at times, it tries to opt for shortcuts whenever possible in order to keep everything going as it is.

It tries to pull out feelings and thoughts from past experiences and also holds up to beliefs for deciding what to do. The brain would not even take any time to verify whether all of them are true or not. It is because, for the brain, you are in extreme danger at the moment that requires to be instantly acted on. Indeed, it is not true, and that is the reason why you will work on it with the help of CBT. In case the brain decides that there is no existence of any immediate danger, the event will keep going for further processing in the portions of the brain that are more recently evolved. Right here, we get the chance to process all forms of complexities of social situations and modern life. It is the place where knowledge and logic live.

It permits us to imbibe new forms of information, make various decisions, and also record the overall outcome of the situations. It is the part of the brain where the training will focus on. In the process of CBT, we will use up the knowledge that is stored right here for overriding automatic thoughts along with the associated feelings from more primitive brain areas. When using the amygdala takes no form of effort, activation of the thinking parts of the brain will use up quite some energy. CBT is all about using up this very portion of the brain even more. Similar to exercising any of your body muscle, the more you keep doing it, the less energy you will need to use. It will definitely take some time and effort to start; however, as you move ahead with the therapy, all of it will become a lot easier.

Feelings Result From Thoughts

All your thoughts help in the creation of feelings. More often, the brain produces emotions almost instantly. It is the place where the idea of a shortcut comes in again. In case you are in a similar kind of situation from your past days, the brain will move ahead and pull out all forms of information along with feelings from all your past experiences. All of that will get applied to the present one. The majority of the time, it is not a problem. However, in the case of depression, it tends to reinforce false assumptions and negative ideas along with the creation of negative emotions. In several cases, your brain will make it look as if all your emotions and thoughts are true. Just because of this, we make up our minds to start reacting to them.

At times this might work out normally; however, at other times, it results in actions that are not much useful. During the sessions of CBT, you will come to learn how you can stop all of these thoughts along with the feelings in order to consider them right before they tend to influence your overall behavior. It obviously takes effort and time as you will be training your brain to perform something that it rarely does. In place of quickly providing you with information for getting through some kind of situation, you will force it to slow down and keep digging deeper for more data of truthful nature. All forms of actions that you tend to take in any kind of situation will rely on all your feelings and thoughts. When you have all forms of positive things present in your mind, you will respond positively.

When there are negative feelings and thoughts in your mind, you will respond negatively. It indicates that you might have two types of reactions to the exact same scenario. Once again, it is something that happens almost instantly. You will learn how to pause right before start acting out and consider how all your actions are going to affect you and others around you. For example, you spill a cup of coffee. We will start with the positive side first. You knock over the coffee mug, and there is coffee all over the table. Your brain will instantly determine that the action is not a real threat to your overall wellbeing. It sends the necessary information to the thinking portions. Your thought will be neutral in such a case – "I spilled coffee on the table that needs to be cleaned, and then I will get one more cup."

With this form of neutral wording, you won't experience much emotion; however, surely not anything negative. In fact, you might find it humorous. All that your action would involve is wipe up the coffee spill and refill the cup again from the kitchen. Now, let us discuss the negative reaction. You spill the coffee on the table. Your brain senses the incident as a threat and immediately sends the necessary information to the amygdala. You start thinking negatively – "I just cannot believe I did this. I am getting clumsy day by day as it will take a long time to get cleaned up." What you have done is set yourself for all kinds of negative emotions – frustration, annoyance, dread, and anger. You would not like to do anything easy and simple, like mopping up the coffee spill. So, you just leave it as it is and along with your empty coffee cup.

The example might seem quite extreme; however, it establishes the connection between feelings, thoughts, and actions, and also how warped our perceptions might turn out to be in case we opt for the negative options. Only because of your negative thoughts, the overall situation seemed a lot bigger than it would be a hard job to handle and clean up the mess. When you suffer from a depressive disorder, all such small tasks might seem impossible for you. The coffee spill will be on the table and stain the same. The remaining coffee in the kitchen will sit as it is and get cold. Now, the overall problem has enhanced and is even tougher to deal with. All of this will invite more negative feelings, thoughts, and actions that just open up the gate to further issues. That is all about the overall cycle of depression.

All your behaviors reinforce your thoughts too. In case you have a positive reaction to the above example, you will reaffirm that the spilled coffee on the table is not a big deal and is only some sort of momentary inconvenience. In case you have a negative reaction, you will further cement how stupid and clumsy you are. You will end up teaching your brain to give up on something when anything bad happens. Even when all such things are not true or realistic, your brain will keep thinking that you are confirming to them and will start informing all your future thoughts. It creates the pathway of shortcuts in the brain. Your feelings, actions, and thoughts develop a cycle. All our negative behaviors will result in further negative thoughts. Some of the physical symptoms that come along with depressive disorder, like lack of motivation and fatigue, will stop you from taking part in positive activities. Thus, it will end up enhancing the level of negative thoughts.

It might turn out to be a daunting task to break through this very cycle; however, if you can successfully do this once, you can see a huge improvement. In fact, correcting only one of the elements of this cycle will improve the others. In the process of CBT, the first emphasis is laid on your thoughts. You will come to learn the ways in which you can determine the negative thoughts and what are the ways in which they seem to be untrue. It is the first big step that you will need to take for altering the way you interact with the external world. It is a natural thing to experience behaviors and emotions of negative nature at times. But people suffering from depression tend to experience them frequently. Any individual can benefit by eliminating a portion of their false beliefs. However, it is more important for all those who tend to have less number of healthy thoughts.

For all such people, the bad nature of incidents tends to stand out more than the good ones and just contributes to depression. The key here is to experience your normal negative emotions but not letting them inform your decisions and actions. Indeed, it will take some amount of time along with work. However, CBT can definitely help you with adjusting your feelings, thoughts, and actions to be easier and positive on yourself. Even at times when you have a bad reaction or an off day, you will be capable of forgiving yourself and allow yourself to learn something new from that situation. You can then move ahead in life without any further issues.

Chapter 5:
How Can CBT Help You?

CBT is a sector of psychotherapy that helps in analyzing the responses that you feel to certain sets of stimuli and then asks the reason why you feel like so. Depression, anxiety, and phobias, when left as it is, can result in irrational responses to various common and simple scenarios because they can very easily lead to altered perceptions of the reality, along with all-around distorted thinking. When properly used, CBT offers patients a different approach that tends to promote healthy and realistic thought. At the core of CBT, there are certain crucial assumptions. The first one is that the thoughts of an individual have some sort of natural influence on his/her actions and behaviors. It indicates that if you are able to alter your thoughts, then you can also alter your actions along with your habitual behaviors for the long-term. We have already discussed this in the last chapter.

In the concept of CBT, nothing in the world takes place in a vacuum, and everything is well connected. The second belief is that, at times, there will be things that cannot be controlled by you. Instead of just obsessing over all such things, CBT focuses on teaching that it is more productive to pay attention to holding onto all those things that can be controlled by you. It helps in ensuring that you maximize the overall effectiveness of the effort that you spend in the best possible way. Let us have a look at an example for understanding the core beliefs of CBT. Suppose two students scored poor marks in an examination. The first student thinks that he/she could have scored better if they were a bit smarter, which indicates that they think of themselves as stupid. All of this, in turn, results in making them feel depressed regarding their prospects in the future. It will also bring in anxious thoughts about completing more amount of work in the class.

Not only has this resulted in him/her taking less responsibility for their grade, but it also ensures that they will not be changing their habits of study in the future. They will have lingering feelings of anxiety and depression always hanging over their head. On the contrary, the second student, who also got poor marks, looks at the grade and thinks that he/she failed to estimate the overall toughness of the examination. Assumption of this type will surely result in disappointment, but for a very short time. It will make him/her confident for their future prospects as they now have a better idea of what they might face in exams and also how to study for the same effectively.

Proper Interpretation Of Everything Around You

One of the primary tasks of the brain is to make sense of the world that is present all around you, along with those things that you experience in life. Your brain keeps taking in a huge stream of data all the time, which indicates that there is something new all the time for interpretation. That is the reason why CBT pays attention to habit creation in order to make sure that the brain properly interprets all the data in a productive way. The key part of any kind of new thought depends on developing various types of assumptions directly based on the stimuli that you have in front of you. For instance, if you notice a man walking towards you with a gun in his pocket, it is quite logical to be cautious of that individual unless and until you are aware of his intentions.

While in the mentioned example, some form of extra safety is certainly warranted. But the water will turn out to be muddier when you start factoring in assumptions made through the filter of either anxiety, fear, or depression. When you factor in all of these, you can easily assume that the person coming towards you has a gun in his pocket, while in actuality, he is only carrying his mobile phone in the pocket. Negative thoughts that often result from misplaced assumptions are termed irrational beliefs. Because of the fact that the brain is trying to bring in more amount of information than it can actually handle, a large chunk of your thoughts that tends to pass through the brain as common experiences will happen on an instinctual and automatic level. Such thoughts are automatic thoughts. We have already discussed how automatic thoughts can turn out to be the prime factors for your anxiety, phobias, or depression.

Automatic thoughts are most of the time dangerous for all those people who are suffering from mental health problems. It is because they tend to occur much before you get the chance to find out whether they are helpful or not. Your brain will accept the flawed thought to be a true one and will also start acting on the same before you can be aware of what exactly is going on. When any of your thoughts are both automatic and irrational, you are most likely to find yourself constantly dealing with various kinds of negative emotions without being aware of the real case.

Maintain Your Emotions And Thoughts On Track

It is of no surprise that thoughts result in emotions, directly or indirectly. In the above-mentioned example of the man with his phone in his pocket, if you assume that he has some sort of negative intentions from the very first, right before you can verify whether they are armed or not, then you will end up generating thoughts that will make it a tough thing to think about the overall situation in a rational way. But in case you can start from the point that you have mistaken the person, your thought will stay clear, and you will be capable of determining what exactly is going on. In the concept of CBT, there are six basic emotions that one needs to be aware of. Each of the emotions might take place with varying degrees of intensity, which will ultimately result in a wider range of feelings in total.

The core emotions are fear, anger, sadness, joy, love, and surprise. As you experience any of the core emotions, even to a very small degree, your body will start experiencing certain physiological effects. For instance, if you are experiencing panic or anxiety that is brought about by phobia of any kind, then the overall effect will be a fight or flight response, accompanied by tension in the muscles, perspiration, and also an increased heartbeat. Regardless of the fact that they might result in some chronic physical responses, emotions often go unnoticed when they occur. It will make them feel just like automatic thoughts in this regard. It is essential to keep in mind that although they might take place without you being aware of the same, they might still affect the overall behavior in a real way.

Change Your Behaviors

Right after you have experienced some sort of emotional reaction and have interpreted a situation, the very last thing that takes place in response to the overall situation is often done through the expression of certain types of behaviors. While this entire process keeps taking place continuously, all those things that are processed are generally very mundane that can warrant additional action. In case you are suffering from some sort of mental health issue, the process will be skewed, and all the behaviors will hurt more than they can actually help. For instance, if we bring back the two students with poor marks from the previous example, they might want to talk about their bad grades with a close friend. However, when both of them call up their friend, their friend does not pick up their call. The first student, who is already in a very poor mental state, could take the missed call as the starting of all possible worst-case scenarios.

He might think their friendship is in danger, or his friend does not consider him to be someone anymore. All of this will lead to further negative emotions and might even destroy a strong friendship. On the other hand, the second student will understand that his friend must be busy and will surely call back when he is free. It won't take much amount of analysis to determine which reaction is more helpful overall.

Consideration Of Core Beliefs

The thoughts that you will have because of any given situation will always be based on your core beliefs. The core belief of every person is going to be different as they depend on past experiences. It also determines how you will interact with the world present around you by default. Your core beliefs can either be negative or positive and will include these:

- People are born good

- People are born deceitful

- Everything will work in the way it should

- The world has no form of justice

- The world is a safe place in general

Only because of the fact that core beliefs develop based on your experiences does not indicate that they will reflect the way the world accurately works. While this might be true for every one of us to varying degrees, it will be specifically true for you in case you are dealing with any kind of mental issue on top of your personal biases that will definitely come along while living a normal life. Well, you can think of the core beliefs as a kind of filter that all your thoughts pass through right before they can result in emotions, actions, or both.

For example, if one of the core beliefs is that no one would truly love you, then even if you try to spend some great time with your friend, your core beliefs will be filtering that experience negatively. It will result in you assuming that he/she is spending time with you only because they feel sorry for you because you must be a burden on everyone around you.

Being Aware Of Cognitive Distortions

All those core beliefs that tend to do more harm than good often reinforce themselves via thought patterns of negative nature. It results in additional negative emotions along with more negative thoughts eventually. The cycle will keep repeating itself. Cognitive distortions of this nature are quite common in people who are suffering from anxiety, depression, or phobias. They tend to manifest themselves in various harmful ways. The first one is by seeing the worst in every possible situation. In case the situation is completely positive, people with cognitive distortions will try to minimize the overall importance of the situation. But if the situation is completely negative, they will not even waste a minute blowing the same completely out of proportion. For instance, your boss is pointing out all your good work to the higher authority at the time of a meeting; however, you are already preoccupied with the event when you spilled some coffee on yourself in the middle of the meeting that you cannot focus on the good.

It is somewhat similar to a habit that people suffering from anxiety, depression, or phobias experience, which is called catastrophizing. It is the act of assuming the worst is going to take place all the time when a great opportunity of your choice comes to force. It is more or less like cognitive distortion of overgeneralization which makes it easier to extend the big results from small issues. It is a dangerous thing when it gets combined with the distortion of magical thinking. It will result in creating links between all those events that are disparate. Also, it might result in causing additional issues, which, when paired up with personalization, can distort events so that it can make things look like you are the one responsible for all those things that are not within your reach. Another common cognitive distortion is mind reading. It makes it an easy task to assume that you completely understand what others are thinking.

It might be the case that you have no form of evidence that it is the case. Fortune telling also works on the same principle and gets applied to events in place of others. Lastly, emotional reasoning can make the task of assumption quite easy that how your emotions are actually making you feel is only a reflection of the world around you at large.

Chapter 6:
Learning To Set Goals

"I need to get this task done," "I want to get in shape as soon as possible," or "I want to be happy in life by bringing balance." All such types of statements are quite common for all of us. Most of us are good at the identification of the changes that we actually want to see in the course of our lives. Before you start with the process of CBT, you will need to make up your mind regarding what you actually want from the same. In case you have chosen this book, the chances are high that you are facing problems with depression or other mental health issues. Your goal is to reduce the intensity of all these. But for succeeding, you will require to be more specific. What do joy and happiness mean to you? What do you think of success? How do the symptoms of depression tend to affect your life? What would your life look like in case the roadblocks get cleared? CBT focuses on journaling a lot. So, the first section of your journal will include all your goals.

The end goal can be long-term or short-term. Either way, you will break them further into several smaller steps that can be accomplished. Try to set a date or deadline for accomplishing each of the steps. The main idea here is to make yourself ready for success. Set up goals for progressing in life; however, provide yourself a proper time for doing so. Trying to push yourself in the direction of your goals too hard might result in frustration and disappointment. It will ultimately result in a negative mindset. Provide yourself enough time along with resources to achieve what you actually want.

When Is Goal Setting Considered To Be Useful?

Setting goals might turn out to be useful in several aspects of life. For instance, saving up money for trips, looking for a new job, getting started with a new hobby, and many others. But goal setting might also turn out to be useful when you try to address difficulties with your behaviors and emotions. It is taken to be a great tool that is used extensively in the process of CBT. For example, an individual suffering from a depressive disorder, who has also isolated himself/herself from others, can work in collaboration with their therapist in the direction of a steady goal for increasing the number along with the strength of friendships. An individual suffering from excessive anxiety due to their job can work with their CBT therapist to explore other sectors of career or take out some time to relax. As the strategy of goal setting is widely used in the process of CBT, a therapeutic approach of this nature might turn out to be useful for those people who face difficulties in meeting their goals, regardless of what goal it might be.

The easiest way of beginning with goal setting is by determining the areas of your life that you would like to work on. What are the things that are bothering you the most at the moment? After you have successfully determined the area, try to consider your latest experiences with the same. For instance, one of the worries of life could be the amount of money you have saved and your difficulties in paying bills. Your latest experiences could be spending more, losing your job, or have some unexpected expenses crop up. All of these will make you lose all your savings, and you might even fail to pay your bills. You might make up your mind that your only goal now is to pay bills on time every month.

SMART Goals

SMART acts as an important part in identifying the proper goals and steps. The full form stands for:

Specific: All your goals are required to be properly defined. "Opt for my dream job" is a vague goal and will, therefore, be tough to attain. In place of that, you will need to make it something specific like, "I want to work as a reputed journalist in the top newspaper of the city within two years." When your goals are not specific enough, it will make it tough for you to work on the same, resulting in hopelessness and frustration without any sense of purpose.

Measurable: Your steps and goals need to be something that can be measured properly. For instance, if your goal is to get trained for a marathon, one of the steps might be to run every day. You will have to make it something that you can keep track of, like "run four days every week." You can then check off all those days when you completed the goal and track your progress. In case your set goals are not at all measurable, you won't be able to maintain a track of working towards them or determine how and where you have improved.

Achievable: It goes back to setting yourself up for success. All you set goals need to be attainable with the resources you have. For instance, winning a lottery is not that achievable. It is almost impossible to take steps in the direction of the same or just guarantee that you will win. Opting for unachievable goals will only result in disappointment.

Relevant: All the stepping step goals need to be relevant to the long-term and main goals. Any opportunities that you run after, any skills that you gain, or any kind of action that you opt for should always direct you to the large goal. Learning how to play a new musical instrument is a good goal; however, it is not relevant at all to the primary goal of making two new friends this year. Any kind of irrelevant step will just add up to the time that it will take to reach the primary goal. Try to set other goals aside or keep them in store to work on once you have successfully completed the one that you have in hand.

Timely: It can indicate two different things. First, you will need to set all your goals during a good time so that you can work on them. Starting with a veggie garden is a great goal but not something to work on during the winter season. Another great example is to set your goal to work out more, which cannot be done as you just had knee surgery. Always try your best to set yourself up for a win. Setting all those goals that cannot be accomplished currently will lead to more amount of frustration and negativity. It will only leave you doing nothing at all when you could have used the time for something else. Second, you will need to develop a timeline by which you will be completing all your goals. It will provide you with focus along with a great way to keep track of your progress.

The Four-Step Method

The approach of goal setting that you will find in this section is based on the methods that are used in the process of CBT. But the approach can turn out to be useful for anyone.

- **Identification of goals:** It might sound quite simple; however, identifying a clear and proper goal is always very important. For getting started, you will need to ask yourself, "What is the actual goal of my life?"

- **Identification of starting point:** After you are done with the identification of your goal, you will need to take

58

stock of the present state of everything with respect to your goal. Be honest and ask yourself, "What is the position of everything now?"

- **Identification of steps:** It might be an easy thing to forget that achieving a goal can be rarely accomplished in one single step. You will have to break down the set goal into various small chunks simply by identifying all those steps that it would need right from the starting point to the ending line of your goal. Ask yourself, "How can I break this down into smaller pieces for making it seem more achievable?" You will need to make sure that all such steps are small in size. Keep in mind that opting for smaller steps is more achievable in comparison to the bigger ones. When you succeed with the small steps, it will help in keeping up your level of motivation towards your goal.

  Try asking yourself, "What would be the very first step in attaining the goal?" followed by "Now, what would be the next step?" You will need to keep going like this unless you have got a complete route map for attaining your goal. You will have to pay more attention to the starting steps and also pay attention to the roadblocks that you might face on your way. You will have to be mindful of determining the obstacles that might come in the middle.

- **Getting started:** The last and final step is to start with the very first step that you have decided in your plan of action.

Are you enjoying this book? If yes, it would be great if you leave a quick review on Amazon, it is really important to me, thank you!

Chapter 7:
CBT For Dealing With Depression

Depression or depressive disorder is the most common mental health issue that can be widely found in any corner of the world across any age group. Indeed, it can be found in any age; however, adolescence till early adulthood is the most common age. It has been found that depression can be found in women twice that in men. In general, depression gets presented with a wide array of cognitive, behavioral, emotional, occupational, interpersonal, and social symptoms. Depressive disorder might have variable severity, and for some, it might turn out to be a form of recurrent illness. It can also be found side by side with other types of mental health conditions, anxiety disorders, phobias, and many others.

CBT Contradictions

There is no form of definite contradiction in relation to CBT. However, it is often stated that people with chronic comorbid disorders because of personalities, like antisocial personality disorders and subnormal intelligence, are quite tough to be managed and treated with CBT. Special training along with expertise might be required in order to treat such patients. In fact, patients suffering from chronic depression besides suicidal instincts are hard to be managed by CBT alone. For such patients, additional medications might be prescribed before starting with the process of CBT. But there is a wide range of advantages of CBT in relation to depression.

- It is widely used for reducing the intensity of the symptoms as a form of independent treatment or, at times, with some medications.

- It can be used for addressing various psychological problems, like marital discord and job stress, which might readily dedicate to the symptoms of depression.

- It is quite effective in the modification of underlying beliefs that allow depression to persist.

- It helps in enhancing adherence to recommend other types of medical treatments.

- It is effective in reducing the chances of recurrence.

Treatment Choices

Typically, CBT is performed on an OPD basis that involves a series of planned sessions. Each session lasts for about fifty minutes or a maximum of one hour. The timeframe of the session depends entirely on the suitability of the patient and the therapist. In some situations, CBT might be delivered in inpatient settings which involve usual treatments as well. For instance, patients with risk of self-harm, patients with several medical comorbidities, patients with severe depression, and others.

Using CBT Depending On Overall Severity

Various trials have shown the benefits of combined treatment in order to treat the symptoms of depressive disorder. Indeed, it is a bit costly in comparison to other forms of treatment; combined therapy will deliver you with the overall cost-effectiveness by preventing relapses. The total number of sessions needed will rely on the patient's responsiveness. Also, your therapist might also include several booster sessions between the timeframe of the first month and the twelfth month in accordance with the clinical necessities.

Nature of depression: Mild

Total number of sessions: 6 – 12

Nature of depression: Moderate

Total number of sessions: 7 - 16

Nature of depression: Severe

Total number of sessions: 16 or more than that

Nature of depression: Chronic and recurrent depression

Total number of sessions: More than 16, in addition to booster sessions for about two years

While treating depression with CBT, there is a general outline that gets followed.

- Goal setting

- Mutual agreement after defining problems by the patient and the therapist

- Modification of necessary thoughts and behaviors

- Explaining and familiarizing the patients with the model of CBT

- Prevention of relapse

- Applying new skills and strategies in therapy sessions

- Ending the overall therapy

Model Of Cognitive Depression

According to cognitive theory, we are not influenced by our life events. We tend to get influenced by the view that we all have on the events. It means that differences in maladaptive thinking processes and negative appraisal of life events result in various types of dysfunctional cognitive reactions. Cognitive dysfunctions of this nature are the ones responsible for the initiation of other affective and behavioral symptoms.

- Stable internal information structure that is formed during early life that also includes core belief about oneself.

- Intermediate information processing and beliefs are interpreted as living rules. They get expressed as "then and if" sentences.

- Automatic thoughts that are related to everyday events. In the case of depression, it reflects the cognitive triad, which is nothing but the negative view of the future, oneself, and the world.

The negative triad is as follows:

- Hopelessness: My future is blank.

- Worthlessness: I am of no worth.

- Helplessness: I am completely helpless.

Effectiveness Of CBT In Treating Depression

CBT is often referred to as the best psychological intervention that is completely based on pieces of evidence for proper treatment of several psychiatric disorders. The overall usage of CBT has been extended recently to psychotic disorders, behavioral medicine, marital discord, stressful situations, and some other conditions. There are various studies that have been conducted to showcase the all-round efficacy of the process in treating depression and its symptoms. In a meta-analysis of fifteen studies, it has been found that CBT is quite effective in treating the symptoms of depression. When used along with other forms of treatments of pharmacotherapy, it can work even better in comparison to pharmacotherapy alone. Additionally, the rate of relapse in patients who are treated with CBT is quite less in comparison to all those who get treated with pharmacotherapy alone.

The treatment guidelines for depression suggest that psychological interventions are very effective and are quite acceptable to be used as a way of treating patients. Psychological interventions are put into use for treating a depressive disorder that generally ranges between mild and moderate. CBT is suggested by most therapists as a treatment option for depression because of its quick resolution capabilities and efficacy.

Patient-Related Factors

There are certain factors related to the patients that can facilitate the overall response to the treatment effectively.

- The main thing that needs to be considered is the psychological mindedness of the related patient. Patients who can effectively understand all their emotions and also label each of them can respond in a much better way to the process of CBT. In fact, there are patients who come to learn all such skills during the course of CBT.

- The intellectual level of the patients also affects the effectiveness of the therapy.

- An important factor that comes into play is the willingness and motivation on the part of the concerned patient. Of course, it is not something that is required from the very beginning. But people who are motivated to analyze their feelings and are all set to opt for several types of homework will always show better responses in comparison to others.

- Another important factor is the preference of the patient. Right after the very first assessment of the patient, who prefers and needs some sort of psychological treatment, can be introduced to CBT. CBT can be provided alone or in combination with certain other treatments depending on the type and severity of depression.

- Patients suffering from chronic depression might need a combination of both CBT and medications.

- Patients who suffer from depression that ranges between mild and moderate can be introduced to the first line of treatment.

- Certain considerations might be required in certain situations – for example, children and adolescents, medical comorbidities, pregnancy, lactation, and many others.

Ending The Process

CBT or cognitive behavioral therapy is a type of therapy that is directed towards the goals and is time-limited as well. So, in the majority of cases, patients are informed regarding the ending of the treatment in advance. It is generally done in these stages:

- Identifying dysfunctional assumptions

- Consolidating learning blueprint

- Preparing for setback

Chapter 8:
Recognizing Cognitive Distortions And Negative Thoughts

The very first step of putting CBT into use is recognizing all sorts of negative thoughts. Well, this might turn out to be quite difficult. They are referred to as the "automatic thoughts" as they tend to spring up without any kind of information regarding how or why. For changing them, you will need to start by determining where all of them come from. Automatic negative thoughts can also be sorted into other categories, called cognitive distortions. Getting knowledge of this will allow you to properly determine the negativity and also find out the root of the same. They are called distortions as they are not based on reality. All of them are thoughts that are produced by the brain automatically, in most cases based on your past experiences or some sort of biased beliefs. Unlike psychoanalysis, in the process of CBT, the primary cause of the cognitive distortions is not that important.

The events that resulted in them have already taken place, and there is no chance of changing them now. But the distortions can be easily challenged and deal with until the mind learns how not to create them. Cognitive distortions are generally exaggerated and negative but convincing. Even when they seem to be true, once you start digging into them, you will come to find out that none of them are based on reality. They tend to serve no form of good purpose and tend to fuel pessimism. It is worth stopping and taking a look at any kind of negative thoughts that tends to cross the mind and find out whether they can fit in any of the below-mentioned categories. Also, there might be some of them that might not just fit into any of the categories. The true test is whether any of the thoughts are based on realistic thinking and whether it serves a positive purpose.

The majority of people tend to suffer from a couple of cognitive distortions. But they are also strongly attached to certain mental disorders like depression. In all those people suffering from depression, cognitive distortions tend to be more prevalent and also impart a greater effect on mental health. Those that are not affected strongly are able to dismiss the thoughts in no time or just do not give them much importance. Try to have a look at the types of cognitive distortions and determine which one might apply to you. Some might readily jump at you or be the ones that you know you already experience. Some might surprise you, but you will come to know something about automatic thoughts.

All-Or-Nothing Thinking

It is also known as black and white thinking or polarized thinking. In this nature of thinking, you cannot find any type of in-betweens. Everything tends to fall to one side or the other of the extreme scale. Everything is seen as black or white and never gray. All of this results in enhanced negativity in the direction of anything on the "not so good" side of the scale and turning away from the middle ground that might be more reasonable. Examples:

- Either hating or loving anyone you meet

- Any situation is either the worst or the best

- Thinking of yourself as either a complete failure or perfect

Overgeneralization

It is the belief that certain instances of something indicate it is a pattern, paying no attention to the life complexities. It is the type of thinking that might result in stereotypes of huge groups of people. But this one is generally on a much smaller scale. It results in negative thinking regarding the perceived pattern. Examples:

- A close friend of yours misses a lunch date with you, so you start thinking he/she will never make it to any kind of commitment.

- You get low marks on a test, so you start thinking of yourself as dumb, and also you won't be able to pass the class.

- Your boss discusses small mistakes on your part, so you start thinking that you are a failure and also you might be fired from the job.

Mental Filter

A person having this type of distortion will try to discount all the positives in order to pay attention to the negatives. When any form of critique is offered, they will take away only the negative comments and keep aside the positive ones. It results in doubt, low self-esteem, and having the belief that others only see all their negative aspects. Examples:

- During a performance evaluation of your work, you tend to focus on a negative comment, despite the presence of various positive ones.

- You only accept the negative comments and what you should change from any critique on the paper you wrote.

- You pay attention to the negative situations with your relationship partner, and despite the wide array of positive situations, you start believing that your relationship is all over.

Discounting The Positives

It is more or less like a mental filter; however, in place of not paying attention to the positives, they are regarded to be false. Distortion of this nature can be damaging particularly, as, despite all sorts of evidence to the contrary, only the negative aspects are seen. Even when the positives are pointed out in the direction of the individual, it will not be enough for convincing them. Examples:

- You got a positive review at work; however, you tend to believe it is because your senior is trying to be diplomatic. You do not deserve it in actuality.

- Whenever you get a compliment from one of your friends, you think they are saying so just to be nice, and not as it is true.

- When you receive any kind of criticism on a project, you tend to believe that the false positive points exist for softening the actual negative ones.

Mind Reading

Mind reading is like jumping right to conclusions. It is when a person assumes that they know everything that the other person is feeling or thinking. We might often pick up body language along with other cues for guessing what other people might feel. However, in mind reading, it goes much beyond the point to be known as psychic. The person who suffers from this tends to believe that people are always thinking negatively about them, without any form of solid evidence. People experiencing this form of distortion tend to believe that other people are always thinking the worst about them, resulting in low self-esteem and doubt. Examples:

- Your boss makes a slight facial expression as you hand him over some report. So, you start thinking he does not like your report and is also upset with what you have done.

- Two individuals standing beside you start laughing. So, you start assuming that they are making complete fun of you.

- A stranger on the bus scowls at you. So, you start thinking that you must have done something that offends them.

Fortune Telling

It is another form of jumping right to conclusions. In this type of distortion, the sufferer keeps predicting the future without any form of evidence, generally in a negative way. It is once again playing psychic and paying attention only to a negative outcome instead of the possibility of a variety of outcomes. Continuously paying attention to the negatives means there is no form of joy in participating in anything and might lead to depression. Examples:

- Your friend decides to go to a movie with you that you have not heard of, and you start assuming that the movie won't be good.

- You assume that the flight might get canceled at the last moment and you won't be able to go for your vacation.

- You see clouds in the sky and assume it will start raining very soon, completely ruining the outdoor party that you decided to go to.

Chapter 9:
How To Challenge Your Negative Thoughts?

Once you start recognizing the negative thoughts for the actual distortions they are, you can start challenging them. After you have maintained the log for quite some time, you will come to find that you are now capable of identifying all your cognitive distortions with minimal effort. When you reach this point, it is now time to figure out why they are not helpful or true. It is termed cognitive reframing or restructuring. Continue to maintain the log of your negative thoughts. But you will also need to start adding certain additional information. You will need to do this as soon as possible so that the overall situation surrounding the entire idea is fresh in mind. You can set up your journal to include the subjects for each of the negative items that you want to challenge. You can either design a table with dedicated columns for each or just leave some blank spaces after each of the thoughts.

It does not really matter the way you decide to write it all out, as long as it is something that you feel comfortable with using frequently. Also, you might not require using all of these for negative thoughts. Try to consider each of your thoughts and select the ones that actually apply. The key here is to put into use your best possible judgment.

Finding Out Whether The Thoughts Are True

It is one of the most important questions that you will need to answer while taking into consideration all your negative thoughts. It applies to all sorts of distortions. Generally, automatic thoughts are not structured on the facts but on opinions, beliefs, or assumptions. But it is quite an easy task for us to accept thoughts as the only reality. For being capable of recognizing all the harmful thoughts for what they actually are, you will have to ensure that you can differentiate facts from opinions. Have a look at the below-mentioned list and try to identify each of them as an opinion or fact.

1. She said that she does not like what I said.

2. I am a really bad person.

3. I am obese.

4. He shouted at me.

5. I failed the test.

6. I am not that attractive like others.

7. All of this will result in a disaster.

8. Everything tends to go wrong in my life.

9. I am a selfish person.

10. I am lazy.

11. There has to be something wrong with my personality.

12. My ears are too big.

13. I did not give the money to that friend which he asked for.

14. I am never going to be loved by someone else.

The entire exercise is quite simple. By looking at the phrases from an analytical and objective view, you will find it easy to differentiate the facts from all the opinions. But when the opinions tend to manifest in mind as automatic thoughts, we start accepting them as the only facts. An essential part of CBT is to learn to examine all your thoughts in the similar disconnected way you view all these. Points 1, 3, 5, 9, and 13 are facts. The rest are opinions. Try to notice that the opinions are filled with negativity. If you try to take the opinions as facts, it might affect your overall mental state in a bad way. The facts here are neutral statements that tend to describe the circumstance or the situation. It is quite a natural thing to have certain opinions on all those things that happen in our lives. The aim here is not to reduce them.

It is all about recognizing all of them for what they actually are and then adjusting all your thinking in case they are negative in nature. Keep in mind that the negative opinions will only be harming your overall mental health. Even when you are in a truly negative situation, thinking about the same in a positive way will surely improve the overall outcome. Indeed, this might be a tough thing to keep in mind when you tend to be in an emotional state of disruptive nature. That is the reason why it is so important to practice the same whenever possible. The more you can train the brain to differentiate between facts and opinions, the easier it will be for you to perform the same when in a hard situation.

It is more or less like muscle memory in relation to sports – once you get used to throwing the ball in a particular way, all your muscles will do the same without the need of you thinking of the same. Another thing that you will have to consider at the time analyzing the truth of any thought is the source. The majority of automatic thoughts come from within the mind. But you might also find some that come from others. It can be anything – a comment regarding you that has engraved in your mind and something that you have accepted to be true. It might also be the reasoning or belief of someone else that you have inherited. In such a case, you will have to think of the person that you think the overall idea came from. How trustworthy you think they are? What was their real intention in all those things said by them? You might find out that some of these individuals are not someone that you can rely on, like as an antagonizer or a person you know who has plenty of faulty assumptions and beliefs.

In the journal, try to write down if your thoughts are opinions or facts. After that, figure out whether they are based on assumption or reality. That alone is a great start; however, you can go ahead and write down the reasoning for each of them. For instance, let us look at the phrase "My ears are too big" from the above-mentioned list. All of us know it is an opinion and not a fact. In order to further expand on the same, you can write, "The proper proportions of someone's face are completely subjective, and everyone in this world come with their own opinions." We can further clarify the same by saying, "No one ever told me that my ears are big. I am just assuming that it is what others might think of my ears."

Finding Out Whether The Thoughts Are Even Useful?

Right after you are done with determining whether a thought is true or not, you will need to think about whether the same is useful or not. Are the thoughts harmful in any way, or are they useful? An example of useful automatic thought is not being capable of finding something that you require and just thinking, "I should have cleaned the table long ago." It can be regarded as a cognitive distortion as it is a 'should' statement and makes you blame yourself and also add up unnecessary guilt. But it might turn out to be useful as now you have realized the necessity to clean the table, and you can gradually start working on the same. Another great way of looking at this is an analysis of cost-benefit. Try to think of the advantages of trusting your distorted thoughts, along with the disadvantages. Now, take into consideration your behaviors and feelings that might stem from either of the choices.

Start comparing the two and figure out which one would win. If you can figure out that the disadvantages tend to outweigh all the advantages, you can easily dismiss that thought. In case the advantages are more than the disadvantages, try to consider why it is so. You might have just uncovered one more goal that you can work on. But you will have to reword the same to make it more positive. There are several automatic thoughts that cannot be considered to be productive in any possible way. Having thoughts like, "I look ugly" won't provide you with any kind of helpful information or ways of improving yourself. It is nothing more than a self-insult that is not at all based on reality. Properly identifying them as such and then writing the same down can help you in dismissing such thoughts. It is a great way to label, discount the positive, be right always, and think magically.

Checking The Evidence

The question applies to the majority of types of distortions. You will need to examine the overall situation along with your thoughts in an objective way. Suppose you are standing in a courtroom and you are putting all your thoughts on trial. Well, roleplaying might seem a bit silly at first; however, it helps in taking one step back and viewing everything in a more objective way. First, opt for the role of the defense attorney and provide evidence for supporting the automatic thought. You might also present no feelings or emotions and only facts. Statements that tend to start with "It seems like.." or "I feel..." will not be accepted. Now switch to the role of the prosecuting attorney. You will now need to provide evidence against your automatic thought. Once again, you will have to keep it as factual as possible.

In the end, act as the judge and make a proper verdict. You will be looking at both sides of the argument and find out where you can find the most compelling evidence. The chances are high that the prosecutor will win, and your thought can be dismissed. By looking at the arguments that are against your automatic thoughts, you can find out how unrealistic they are. At times, human beings will only accept all those information that actually supports their existing beliefs. It is a natural thing; however, it is still a habit that you need to get rid of. The more you practice this, the more you will be able to do the same automatically.

Looking For The Alternatives

You will need to consider certain things for this section. First, what would be the probable alternate way of looking at the present situation? Is there any possible misinterpretation that might have happened? If yes, then how can they be prevented? Try writing down a more neutral or positive way of viewing the scenario. Second, try to think of the ways in which the entire situation would have played out in case you did not have your assumptions or automatic thoughts. If all those ideas never cropped up in your head, how would the entire situation be? Could there be any kind of difference in your behavior? Write in the journal all kinds of alternative scenarios or your ways of thinking. You will have to try your best to be as neutral as you can. It is nothing more than looking at the entire situation in a different way. It will provide you with the needed help to learn what can be done in all such moments and how you can avoid some negative outcomes.

Figuring Out The Worst Possible Case

It is often referred to as 'finishing the script.' In the process of CBT for depression, this process is widely used. It provides help for all those scenarios that include distortions of mind-reading, fortune-telling, and also catastrophizing. Try to think of all those situations that were dreading or the worst way in which any situation might have ended. Try to write down all of that. Well, putting anything on the paper will help you realize that the overall scenario was not that bad as the emotions forced you to believe. Even when it is much less than desirable, you will find out that you have lot more options present in front of you than all your faulty logic indicates you do.

Chapter 10:
Gateway To Positivity

After you start feeling comfortable in challenging all your negative thoughts and might also start doing the same automatically without any need to write them down, you can start replacing them with all kinds of positive thoughts. Just by challenging all your cognitive distortions, you can banish them. You will soon notice a reduction in the frequency and number that you have them. Replacing them with something good is the next big step that you will have to take for reframing your patterns of thinking.

Counteracting With Positive Thoughts

Try to look back at the log of your negative thoughts. Can you figure out any pattern? It might be a thought that keeps reoccurring or various thoughts regarding the same topic. Note down all of these in a brand new list. After you are done with this, counteract each of the thoughts with a positive statement. It needs to be a more positive version; however, try not to stray far from the actual statement. In case that happens, the brain is most likely to think of it as a fact. When you are suffering from chronic depression, your brain will keep you away from feeling better. It will guard all your positive feelings and protect them in place of allowing you to enjoy and experience them. You can regard this as a way of preventing disappointment and hurt. But that is all that helps in keeping the depression cycle going on. Your goal is to break through this cycle in order to start experiencing the great things again.

For example, a reoccurring theme of your negative thoughts is that you are unattractive. The opposing statement should never be something like, "I am the most beautiful creature on this planet." It is because the depressed mind will discard this as unrealistic immediately. In place of such statements, use, "Beauty is different for everyone and subjective. There are several people who actually find me quite attractive, and I also possess various qualities that I love about myself." Indeed, this will provide your mind with all the protective habits to deal with. But the aim is not to contradict it directly. You will have to provide your mind with a new perspective of looking at all types of situations. Try to do this for all those thought patterns that are quite strong.

Changing Self-Talk

One of the primary components of our overall mood is the way we try to talk to ourselves. With your cognitive distortions in action, these statements are quite common – "I am not able to do this" or "I am not capable enough." In order to heal yourself, you will have to alter your way of self-talk. Try to evaluate your self-talk, and determine whether you would say such things to a close friend of yours. The chances are high that you would not. Provide yourself with the permission to be your own best friend. Begin morphing your self-talk into an attitude of positive nature. For example, if you think that you will fail an exam, try to cheer yourself up in the same way as you would have done for a friend. Try to remind yourself that you can still study, you have a proper idea of the material, and you can surely pass the exam. Remember your double standard cognitive distortions. It often gets applied to the way you converse with yourself.

Opting For Positive Affirmations

Even at times when you are not trying directly to switch off a negative thought, you should have positive affirmations in stock that are ready to go. Take some time and write down all forms of good qualities that you think you have in the journal. You can make it broad, like writing down that you are great in studies, or you can also be more specific with situations and scenarios that you have handled in your past. Out of each such thing, try to come up with an easy and simple statement that you can tell yourself. As you write all of these down, you will come to see all those things that are good about you. Having all such affirmations ready in the journal or in your mind will allow you to pull from them whenever you have any requirement of positivity. It is quite easy to get down on ourselves when we are suffering from depression. However, we will have to keep in mind all our good qualities to prevent ourselves from getting dragged into that cycle.

Positive affirmations also indicate talking up to yourself or letting yourself know how great you are. But there is a way in which this might backfire. In case you are excessively outrageous with the statements, you won't actually believe in them, even when you are saying them. It is an essential thing to pay attention to the progress that you are actually making instead of just trying to make yourself sound perfect. "I am successful and happy, and there is nothing that can bring me down" sounds quite false. Your brain might decide not to pay attention to the same, and it might even result in more amount of negativity. In place of that, try to focus on the work. "I am progressing every day and making myself better. I have altered my self-talk for my betterment." It sounds more realistic and also acknowledges the effort that you have actually put in.

Let's have a look at some of the questions that you will answer in your journal for picking up positive affirmations regarding yourself.

- What are the things that I like about myself?

- What are the good qualities that others find in me?

- Can I support others?

- What are the latest compliments that I have received?

- What are the values and morals that I live by?

- What are the things that make me excited?

Practicing Daily Gratitude

It is something that can help you in noticing more number of positives. There are people who write all of these in their journals to make sure that the thoughts are fully formed. It also helps them ensure that they have a full list of all those things that they are truly grateful for. At some time every day, try to write down 3 – 4 things in life that you think you are grateful for. If you decide to do this in the morning, it will let you start your day in a bright way, or if you opt for the evening, it will provide you with a nice way to wrap up the entire day and then properly reflect on the same. Try to opt for the time that works the best for you and make sure you are focused enough while doing so. The items that you think you are grateful for can be anything. It can be large, such as the love of your family members. It can be small as well, like the pastry that you had today after lunch.

The items can focus on your emotions and thoughts or even physical things. In case you are having a bad day, it might be something like, "I am grateful that tomorrow will start soon, and I will get the chance to start over again." Ensure that the entries of your gratitude are a bit different every day. In case they turn out to be repetitive, your mind will start dismissing all such items. You will have to focus on the items truly and the way they tend to make your life even better. Regardless of how simple or small they are, they need to have some sort of effect on you that can improve your day. Let's have a look at some of the questions that you can use for finding positivity and gratitude in life.

- What are the top twenty things that make me happy?

- Is there any problem that I solved successfully on my own recently? Can I describe the solution and the situation?

- What are the things that I did well today?

- Who are those people who have some kind of positive influence on my life, and why?

The primary key to find lifetime positivity is to turn into an optimist. Generally, depression tends to turn us into pessimists – viewing only the negatives all the time and always expecting the worst outcomes. On the other hand, optimists see more of the positives in any possible scenario and consider the negatives as one-off-moments. Being an optimist is all about attributing the good things to our skills, along with the frame of our minds.

Chapter 11:

How To Deal With External Negativity?

You are now aware of the ways in which you can deal with the negativity produced by your mind. With daily practice, you will start getting better, and ultimately you will have a fewer number of negative thoughts. But the chances are high that you might still run into the negativity that is out of your control. It could be people you interact with, situations that you find yourself involved in, or various other events in the world. Although all such things cannot be avoided completely, it is essential for you to have all your defenses right in place so that you can set up healthy barriers. No matter what is the case, we all know certain very negative individuals in our lives. They might be our friends, family members, or our colleagues. You can easily think of a person who is negative and also broadcasts the same often.

There might also be people in your life who are not that negative but can still have certain harmful effects on your mental health. Well, the best possible solution is to stay away from all such individuals; however, that cannot be regarded as an option all the time. Whenever you try to interact with a person who is very pessimistic, keep in mind that they have some kind of unhappiness in their life that they are not able to deal with properly. You will need to approach such individuals with understanding and compassion. You can never be too sure what the reason behind their attitude is. But when someone keeps trying to drain every person present around them, how can you maintain compassion without getting dragged into the doom? There are certain ways in which this can be done.

Resisting The Urge To Assume Or Judge

It is a hard thing to offer compassion to someone when you start assuming that you have them pegged. He is a bad person, she is not worth this, and many other statements are quite common among all of us. Even when it seems a bit unlikely, someone will surely wake up one day and start acting differently. You will have to keep in mind that it is actually possible. When you start thinking negatively, it will surely come out through your body language. A person who is prone to negativity might feel tempted to mirror the same. Try reaching them out with a somewhat positive mindset that you wish they had. Try to expect the best things in them as you can never be too sure when they might surprise you.

Setting And Enforcing Limits

People with a negative attitude who tend to wallow all the time in their problems and who fail to concentrate on the solutions are quite hard to deal with. They desire people to join their all-time pity party so that they get the chance to feel better about themselves. You might feel the pressure to listen to all their complaints as you would not want to be seen as rude or callous. However, there exists a fine line between providing a compassionate ear and getting dragged into emotional drama of negative nature. The drama of this kind can be avoided by setting up limits and distancing yourself when needed. Try to think of it in this way: if a negative individual keeps smoking cigarettes, would you still sit beside that person inhaling all their second-hand smoke? Of course, you would not do this and would try to distance yourself from that person. So, try to go ahead and provide yourself with some room to breathe when you need.

In case distancing yourself is not much possible, another way of setting limits is by asking the person the ways they think of fixing the problems that they keep complaining about. Most of the time, they would either redirect the conversation or just quiet down in a harmonious direction, temporarily.

Responding Mindfully

A reaction is a thoughtless, hot, and in-the-moment bursting of emotions that gets driven by your ego usually. It might last only for some time right before your intuition comes into the picture and provides you with some sort of perspective, or it might direct you to the point where you can act on the same. When you start feeling flustered or angry right after dealing with a person of negative nature that is a sure sign that you have reacted in place of responding mindfully. Trying to respond mindfully will provide you with the feeling that you have handled everything with poise and integrity. Talking of the bottom line, as you encounter a person who comes with a negative attitude, try not to respond to them by throwing back insults at them. You will have to maintain your own dignity by not lowering yourself down to their level. True strength is when you are bold enough to walk away from all kinds of nonsense with your head kept high.

Introducing Lighter Discussion Topics

The negative attitudes of certain people tend to get triggered by certain harmless topics. For instance, negative people might turn into toxic victimizers when someone starts talking about their job. Regardless of what you try to say, they will keep complaining regarding their job. If you try to interject using positive comments, they will try to roll them over with more amount of negativity. All of this might turn into a conversation damper. In case you also find yourself in such conversational situations, and the negative person you are conversing with is stuck on one topic that tends to bring you down, you will have to realize that all their negative emotions are too deeply rooted that cannot be addressed in a one-off conversation. The best bet from your side in such a situation is to bring in a new topic for lightening the mood. Easy and simple things, such as mutual friendships, funny memories, stories of personal success, and any other kind of happy news, can easily lighten a conversation. Try to keep it to all those areas that the negative person feels positive about.

Concentrating On Solutions And Not The Problems

How and where you focus all your attention can determine your overall emotional state. When you try to concentrate only on the problems that you are facing, you develop prolonged negative stress and emotion. As you try to shift all your attention in the direction of actions that can enhance all your circumstances, you can develop a sense of self-efficacy that can reduce stress and yield positive nature of emotions. A similar kind of principle also applies to while dealing with people of negative nature. When you try to fixate on how difficult and stressful their lives are, it will only be intensifying all your sufferings by providing them more amount of power over you.

Try and stop thinking about the ways troubling the person is, and pay attention to all those ways in which you will handle their behavior more positively. It will make you even more effective by

87

placing you on the seat of the driver. It will also help in reducing the stress that you might experience while interacting with such people.

Maintaining Emotional Detachment From The Opinions Of Others Regarding You

Properly maintaining a level of detachment in the emotional sector is important in order to stay away from stress. Not permitting negative individuals to put all the weight of their inadequacies right on your back is essential for your overall happiness and emotional health. Ultimately, it all comes down to the ways you actually value your own self and also believe in yourself. All those people who can manage their lives effectively are the ones who work internally – all those who are aware of the fact that well-being and success come from deep within. People who tend to always deal with negativity works externally in general. In simple terms, they try to blame outside events or other people for all those things that do not or do happen. When you try to derive your sense of self-worth and satisfaction from the opinions of other people, you can no longer be in control of your self-happiness.

When people who are emotionally strong feel good for something that they have done, they won't allow the shallow opinions or remarks of others to take that away from them. In reality, you are never as good as other people say when you succeed, and also, you are never that terrible as they try to tell you whenever you lose. What is important is all those things that you have learned, and also what you are trying to do with the same.

Letting Go Of The Desire To Alter The Negative Tendencies Of Others

There are some people whom you can help by setting up a good example, and there are people you can't. Try to identify the difference, and it will allow you to maintain the equilibrium. Do not allow yourself into the tactics of the emotional blackmailers and manipulators by trying your best to control what is not within your control – the behavior of others. You can never change others, and it will be foolish of you to try. As you try to change others, they will resist and will keep being the same. When you try not to change them, they start changing in a miraculous way. Also, trying to change what is not within your control will invite negativity in life.

Chapter 12:

Improving Your Life Everyday

CBT takes some time along with some great work for showing results. But it is worth all the effort. Besides all the steps that we have already gone over, there are certain other things that can be done on your side for easing the overall journey and also take more care of yourself. You will come across certain exercises and activities in this chapter that provides you with the needed help to deal with depression in the best possible way.

Journaling

We have already discussed a number of times the importance of journaling in the previous chapters. Maintaining a journal is the best way of being on track and also improving further. Try to continue your log of negative thoughts. You might not need to use them that much, but still, it is important to keep an eye on all sorts of negativities and also challenge them. In general, journaling also helps in relieving stress and also enhances the condition of mental health. One of the most basic types of a journal is opting for a diary. It is nothing more than a record of your entire day. It can concentrate on all types of events, your feelings regarding them, or even a mixture of both. Typically it is done during the end of the day when all your memories are fresh. It is a superb way of reflecting on your entire day and processing your emotions.

Mindfulness And Meditation

There are people who are quite skeptical regarding meditation until and unless they opt for it. It has gained huge popularity in recent years, and it has been proved to help with mental illness and stress. One of the simplest ways of starting is opting for mindfulness. It is all about noticing your feelings and thoughts and then trying to acknowledge them properly. Take out some quiet time and just sit back to find out what exactly is going through your mind. What are the feelings that you are having at this moment? What is it that you can feel? Which kind of physical sensations are present? After you have successfully established what is going on inside you, try to pay attention to your breathing. Do not try to change it; listen to it and try to pay attention to the air going out and coming in. Allow your mind to relax and keep an eye only on breathing.

In case your mind starts wandering, or something else pops up, gently guide your mind back to breathing. Try not to scold yourself or question your thoughts. You can also opt for setting a timer in order to ensure the time for which you want to practice mindfulness, or you can keep doing the same until you feel relaxed. Mindfulness can be practiced at any time of the day, as many times you want. Take your time to notice and try to take in all the good as you deal with your regular businesses. Whether you opt for meditation on your own or try to concentrate on breathing for some time, all of it can be quite helpful. Trying to force yourself into all your present sensations that you are feeling can help in pulling you out of the dark in your mind and ground you in the present more.

Automatic Writing

As we have already discussed in reference to journaling, writing can act as a superb tool in order to deal with depression and stress. The act of writing out all those things you have in mind gets it out of your mind and places it right in front of you so that you can analyze the same in a better way. Automatic writing is the habit of writing anything that comes to your mind and not trying to stop. Generally, it is done by setting up a timer and then write for a fixed time period. To start with, you can opt for a shorter period of time, like a maximum of five to ten minutes. The very first time when you do this, you will surely find yourself pausing a lot. Just do not stop writing. Even when your mind feels blank, try to write done something like, "I do not have any idea what to write." The aim is to keep writing non-stop till the timer goes off.

Opting for this will allow you to dig out every thought in your mind and also provide you with a chance to acknowledge them. Even when you try to examine all your thoughts purposefully, there will still be something that will hide. Without any option to stop, just thinking about what to write will allow you to drag everything into the bright light.

Behavioral Experiments

It is quite an interesting experiment that will allow you to find out what motivates you and what kind of mind frame works the best for you. It is something not meant for the early stages of CBT. You will have to wait until and unless you are well aware of all your weaknesses and the ways you can counteract them. For this, try to think of any situation for which you need more amount of motivation. It can be anything like working harder, or anything more specific, like getting done with a project on time. Try to come up with the negative as well as positive thoughts that might motivate you to put the effort in. After you have thought of them, you will need to put all of them into action. One day, try to use the negative enforcements and find out how close you can get to reach the goal. Try out a positive idea the next day. You will now need to compare both the results and find out which one worked the best for you.

Chapter 13:
Considering Alternate Outcomes

All of us are the sum total of all our experiences, no matter they are negative, positive, or neutral. All of that not only comes with the power of altering us at the moment but also comes with the potential of shaping everything that tends to come after them, no matter we realize them or not. All of us come with our own set of unique stories, and your story will be a sum total of all those chapters that your life has till now included. No matter what it seems like at the moment, your story is sad and traumatic as well as much it is transformational and positive. Your story develops the core of who you really are and also helps in determining the way you try to present yourself in front of the whole world. No matter you realize this or not, you keep telling your story every day to yourself and also to all those you meet.

Every conversation that you have tends to reflect some of the aspects of your story and also your past experiences.

How Stories Are Developed

Everything that you experience daily gets filtered through all your senses which results in the generation of certain types of negative or positive feelings. The feeling, in turn, triggers a kind of thought which gets related to an emotion that allows the mind to tag the experience as positive or negative, right before getting more specific on the same. As all of these tend to pile up, the brain can look back at them and also assign some sort of broader meaning to all the experiences. All kinds of meanings that you find from your personal experiences are the threads that create the tapestry of the story as a whole. As you try to interpret the story using a negative filter, you will result in developing a new form of limiting beliefs regarding yourself that will surely hold you back in your future. The limiting beliefs might get manifested in several ways along with thoughts like:

- I am stupid.

- I am not deserving enough to enjoy happiness.

- Regardless of what I do, it is never going to be enough.

- I am never going to be good enough.

From all such limiting beliefs arise pain, fear, and suffering that will ultimately make it difficult for the positive emotions to breakthrough.

Getting Stuck In A Loop Of Negativity

Try to think of the last time when you allowed self-doubt and fear to stop you from opting for a positive step in the direction of an essential goal. The behavior of this kind is a classic example of self-sabotage and is most likely some kind of attempt by the subconscious to prevent you from dealing with a case that comes with the potential of reinforcing negativity in your story. Subconscious drives of this nature are termed unconscious drivers and are generally the result of unresolved emotions of any kind. All of this will develop mental barriers that will keep you stuck in the same place for a long time.

Determining The Changing Points

While there are people who might not have any kind of hard time thinking of the turbulent times of their life that they might not have treated in a great way, for others, the split might not be that dry and cut. It does not indicate that they do not have any kind of negative stories in life. But it is just that they might be harder to get uncovered. In case you are facing difficulties in picking out all your negative stories, the very first thing that you will have to do is to determine some time when you can sit all by yourself and just reflect. There might be three types of negative stories that could hold you back in life – stories regarding yourself, stories regarding your friends, and stories regarding the state of the whole world. As you try to consider every sphere of the stories, try to think of the progress that has already been made in CBT so far. You will come to determine the biggest hurdles, and you will also come to find out all those negative stories that need to be looked at once more.

Rewriting The Story

Things are not required to be like this all the time; after all, you are in charge of your own story. Knowing that you have got the power to alter the narrative and changing it in actuality are two completely different things. But determining the perfect place to start from might turn out to be tricky, specifically when you have a huge collection of memories to select from. One of the best places to start is by considering all the ways in which you interpreted all the previous experiences. There are two primary types of interpretations, those that tend to generate a sense of helplessness and those that generate a sense of empowerment. You will always get a choice when it is about determining the way you are going to interpret the story and all those things that happened to you. You can either decide to concentrate on the negatives that will surface all the pain and suffering. Or you can opt for the positive of any situation that will fill your world with joy and happiness.

To rewrite the story, you will have to look hard on all the previous chapters of your life and find out the points where you think fate conspired against you for leaving you at a worse place than you actually thought of. Do you still have some grudge against your boss for not giving you the promotion? Are you still attached emotionally to a previous relationship? The list will keep going on and will also amount to more with time. As you look back at your story, in case you find that you are still holding to very old resentments, you will have to seriously consider what it might be costing you in the long-term. As you look back at past moments, try to consider all those things that you came to learn from the experiences or the way they improved you as a whole.

If you can try to think of the situation in this very way, you will be on the right track to change everything as a positive instead of a negative event. Doing so will make it easier for you to look for the opportunities presented by all your past challenges, and you will come to view them in a new light. Always remember, everyone's story includes hardship. The only possible thing that can make your story different from others is how you try to define the same.

Chapter 14:
Commonly Asked Questions

CBT is quite a common and famous treatment option for depression and mental health issues today. But most people have a certain set of questions right before they can start with the treatment procedure. Also, it is a great thing to get everything cleared from the very first before you opt for something new. So, here are some commonly asked questions regarding CBT that will surely help you to get started with the same.

What Is The Theory Behind CBT?

Cognitive behavioral therapy is completed based on the cognitive model, which says that the way we perceive various situations tends to influence the way we feel emotionally. For instance, an individual going through this might think, "All of this sounds great! It has all that I have been looking for so long." The person feels happy. On the other hand, another individual might think of this like, "Indeed, this sounds great; however, I am not sure whether I can do this or not." The second person feels discouraged and sad. So, it is not the situation that tends to directly affect the way a person feels emotionally, but their thoughts in that very situation. When we are distress, we cannot think of anything clearly, and our thoughts get distorted in one way or the other.

CBT helps people in identifying all their distressing thoughts and also helps in evaluating the extent of the authenticity of the thoughts. In this way, people can learn how distorted thinking can be changed. As we start to think in a more realistic way, we feel better. The emphasis can also be found on problem-solving and opting for behavioral change.

What Is Needed To Get Ready For The Therapy?

One of the first steps is to set up goals. Try to ask yourself, "How would I want myself to be different as I end the therapy?" You will have to think in detail regarding all the changes that you would really want at home, at work, in all your relationships with your friends, colleagues, family members, and others. Try to think of the symptoms that have been actually bothering you and which are the ones that you want to eliminate or reduce. You will have to think of other various areas of life that you would like to improve – cultural or spiritual or intellectual interests, reducing all your bad habits, increasing the duration of exercise, learning new skills of interpersonal development, improving skills of management at home or at work, and many others. Your CBT therapist will provide you with the needed help to evaluate and also refine all these goals so that you can be sure of the goals that you can work on your own and which are the ones that you would need help with.

What Is The Duration Of The Therapy?

The decision about the overall length of the therapy would depend on the goals. It gets decided both by the patient and the therapist. You will get a rough idea regarding the duration after the first or second session. Some patients might get help by only six to eight sessions, whereas others might need some months.

How To Make The Best Use Of The Therapy?

One of the best ways of doing so is by preparing yourself carefully for every session by thinking of those things that you have learned in the last session and then summing them up to discuss in the upcoming session. Another way is to make the therapy a part of your daily life.

How To Know If The Therapy Is Working Properly?

The majority of patients can notice a reduction in their related symptoms within one month of therapy only if they attend the sessions properly. You can also have a look at the scores of the objective tests that you will start after the third week of your therapy.

Conclusion

Thank you for making it through to the end of the *Cognitive Behavioral Therapy for Depression*; let's hope it was informative and was able to provide you with all of the tools you need to achieve your goals, whatever they may be.

CBT comes with the power of changing your life. In fact, it is regarded as one of the building stones of modern-day psychological care. As long as you have a functioning mind, CBT will work for you. But one thing that you will have to keep in mind is that it needs time, and you will have to be patient with the overall process. You will have to pay close attention to all those things that are currently going on in life and also the way you think. You will need to do all these steps by step. There is good news for you – the longer you can do it, the better results you will get.

Just keep going with your journal, and follow all the suggestions and tips that you have found in this book. Try to watch out for all the lapses and be back on track without getting any bad feelings. Depression alters the way your mind works; however, now you have got the tools to change the same for your own good.

Finally, if you found this book useful in any way, a review on Amazon is always appreciated!

Printed in Great Britain
by Amazon